RIVER

Sean Callery

Consultant: David Burnie

KINGFISHER

NEW YORK

KINGFISHER
LONDON & NEW YORK

Copyright © Kingfisher 2012
Published in the United States by Kingfisher,
175 Fifth Ave., New York, NY 10010
Kingfisher is an imprint of Macmillan Children's Books, London.
All rights reserved.

Distributed in the U.S. and Canada by Macmillan, 175 Fifth Ave., New York, NY 10010

Library of Congress Cataloging-in-Publication data has been applied for.

ISBN: 978-0-7534-6740-4

Kingfisher books are available for special promotions and premiums.
For details contact: Special Markets Department, Macmillan,
175 Fifth Ave., New York, NY 10010.

For more information, please visit www.kingfisherbooks.com

Printed in China
1 3 5 7 9 8 6 4 2
1TR/1211/WKT/UNTD/140MA

The publisher would like to thank the following for permission to reproduce their material. Every care has been taken to trace copyright holders. However, if there have been unintentional omissions or failure to trace copyright holders, we apologize and will, if informed, endeavor to make corrections in any future edition.

top = t; bottom = b; center = c; left = l; right = r

All artwork Stuart Jackson-Carter (Peter Kavanagh Art Agency)

Cover c Getty/NGS; cover tl Alamy/B. E. Eyley; cover tcl Naturepl/Colin Seddon; cover tcr Shutterstock/S. Cooper Digital; cover tr Shutterstock/S. J. Watt; back cover t Shutterstock/alslutsky; back cover c Shutterstock/Cosmin Manci; back cover b Shutterstock/Tatiana53; page 1 Shutterstock/Brian Lasenby; 2 Shutterstock/Hintau Aliaksei; 3t Shutterstock/Gert Ellstrom; 3b Shutterstock/thieury; 4tr Shutterstock/Gary Unwin; 4bl Alamy/Leo Kanaka; 4br Shutterstock/Bluerain; 4–5c Murray Robbins; 5tl Shutterstock/Image Focus; 5cr Shutterstock/Soyka; 5bc Shutterstock/Paul Cowan; 5br Shutterstock/contax66; 6bl Naturepl/Jane Burton; 6tr Travis Tuten/Florida Wildlife Conservation; 7tl Shutterstock/Corneliu LEU; 7tr Shutterstock/Jakez; 7ct Shutterstock/Corneliu LEU; 7c Photoshot/Nigel Downer; 7cb Canstock; 7br Shutterstock/Tatiana53; 7br Shutterstock/Gualberto Becerra; 7br Shutterstock/Jakez; 8bl Naturepl/Gerrit Vyn; 8tr Alamy/David Hosking; 8br Photolibrary/OSF; 9tl Getty/Panoramic Images; 9tr Shutterstock/CLM; 9ct Shutterstock/Mariusz S. Jurgielewicz; 9c Shutterstock/John A. Anderson; 9b Naturepl/Gerrit Vyn; 9br Shutterstock/Paul Cowan; 9br Shutterstock/Nikita Tiunov; 9br Thesupermat/Wikipedia; 9br Shutterstock/Vladimir Daragan; 10bl Biopix; 11tr Shutterstock/camellia; 11ct Shutterstock/SimonG; 11c Shutterstock/Bill Kennedy; 11cb Photoshot/NHPA; 11cb Photoshot/NHPA; 11br Shutterstock/Lim Yong Hian; 11br Shutterstock/Susan Montgomery; 12bl Frank Lane Picture Agency (FLPA)/Kevin Schafer/Minden; 13tl Naturepl/Kevin Schafer; 13tr Alamy/Prisma; 13ct Gregory Ochocki; 13cb Photolibrary/Bios; 13br Shutterstock/Eduardo Rivero; 13br Shutterstock/guentermanaus; 14l Naturepl/Andy Sands; 14br Photolibrary/OSF; 15tl Alamy/Martin Fowler; 15tr Shutterstock/cami; 15ct Photolibrary/OSF; 15c Shutterstock/Mr Green; 15cb Shutterstock/Milena; 15bl Alamy/Wildlife GmbH; 15br Shutterstock/Dave Green; 15br Photolibrary/Bios; 16l Alamy/Peter Arnold Inc.; 16tr Alamy/blickwinkel; 16br Alamy/blickwinkel; 17tl Photolibrary/Bios; 17tr Shutterstock/Blacqbook; 17ct Shutterstock/Ingrid Prats; 17c Getty/NGS; 17bc Photolibrary/Bios; 17bl Corbis/Visuals Unlimited; 17br Shutterstock/Vasiliy Koval; 17br Shutterstock/Antoni Murcia; 18l Naturepl/Eric Baccega; 18tr Science Photo Library/Leonard Lee Rue III/Leonard Rue Enterprises; 18br FLPA/Yva Momatiuk & John Eastcott; 19tl Shutterstock/oksana.perkins; 19tr Shutterstock/Soyka; 19ct Shutterstock/Laura Duellman; 19c Shutterstock/Lukich; 19bc Shutterstock/Dennis Donohue; 19bl Naturepl/Eric Baccega; 19br Shutterstock/Sally Scott; 19br Shutterstock/oksana.perkins; 19br Shutterstock/Steve McWilliam; 20l Naturepl/Simon Colmer; 20tr Shutterstock/Eric Etman; 20br FLPA/Foto Natura Stock; 21tl FLPA/Jurgen & Christine Sohns; 21tc Shutterstock/Darkpurple; 21tr Shutterstock/Kuttelvaserova; 21ct Shutterstock/Eric Etman; 21c Shutterstock/Sinelyov; 21bc Photolibrary/Imagebroker; 21bl FLPA/Foto Natura Stock; 21br Shutterstock/Stuart Monk; 21br Shutterstock/Cosmin Manci; 21br Shutterstock/Videowokart; 22l FLPA/Rene Krekels; 22tr Photolibrary/Peter Arnold Inc.; 22br FLPA/Rene Krekels; 23tl Naturepl/Stephen Dalton; 23tr Shutterstock/Yanfei Sun; 23tc Naturepl/Mark Yates; 23c FLPA/Thomas Marent/Minden; 23bc Shutterstock/WitR; 23bl FLPA/Rene Krekels; 23br Shutterstock/Pavel Mikoska; 23br Shutterstock/phdwhite; 24l Naturepl/Andrew Parkinson; 24tr FLPA/Michael Callan; 24br Photolibrary/Bios; 25tl Naturepl/Kim Taylor; 25tr Shutterstock/Elenamiv; 25tc Getty/Dave King/DK Images; 25c Photolibrary/Ludwig Werle/Picture Press; 25bc Photolibrary/Ludwig Werle/Picture Press; 25bl FLPA/Dickie Duckett; 25br Shutterstock/slowfish; 25br Shutterstock/S. Cooper Digital; 25br Shutterstock/vaklav; 26l FLPA/Paul Hobson/Holt; 26r Photoshot/NHPA; 26br Naturepl/Colin Seddon; 27tl FLPA/Imagebroker; 27tr Shutterstock/olinchuk; 27ct Shutterstock/Steve Byland; 27c Shutterstock/S. Cooper Digital; 27bc Shutterstock/Reinhold Leitner; 27bl Alamy/Lee Dalton; 27br Shutterstock/photocami; 27br Shutterstock/Graeme Dawes; 27br Shutterstock/S. Cooper Digital; 27br Shutterstock/MarkMirror; 30tl Shutterstock/Ken Tan; 30bl Shutterstock/alslutsky; 31tr Shutterstock/hfuchs; 31br Shutterstock/alsutsky; 32tl Shutterstock/Vitaly Titov; 32tr Shutterstock/Cosmin Manci

Contents

Introduction 4

Rivers of South America
Catfish 6
Cormorant 8
Piranha 10
River dolphin 12

Rivers of North America
Mayfly 14
Brook trout 16
Grizzly bear 18

Ponds of Europe
Great pond snail 20
Great crested newt 22
Little grebe 24
Otter 26

A European pond food web 28
Glossary and websites 30
Index 32

Introduction

Rivers and ponds are freshwater habitats for many plants and animals. Rivers carry water from hills and mountains down to seas or lakes. Ponds are home to animals that need to live in still water.

Some animals live in the water, others at the water's edge, and some come to drink. They must all eat to live. The list of who eats who is called a food chain.

Next, there are plant-eating animals, such as beavers, that eat tree bark, twigs, and leaves. These creatures are called consumers because they eat other living things.

Plants, such as reeds, water lilies, moss, and algae, make their own food using energy from the Sun. They are called producers and are first in a food chain.

Then there are more consumers, which catch and eat animals and insects. A kingfisher is one of these. It lives beside rivers, hunting and eating fish.

This book takes you through two river food chains and one pond food chain in different parts of the world. You will learn about the life cycles of 11 animals: how they are born, grow, reproduce, and die.

At the top of a food chain is a predator that is so big, strong, and fast that no other animal can catch it. This spot-billed pelican, which mostly eats fish, is a top predator.

Catfish

Sailfin catfish live in the rivers of the Amazon basin in South America. They scrape algae from logs and rocks with their large sucker mouths. They also eat plants.

1 The male fish digs a deep burrow in the riverbank, below the water's surface. This will be a nesting tunnel.

2 The female lays thousands of eggs about 3 feet (1m) inside the tunnel. The male fertilizes and then guards them. He keeps the eggs healthy by moving the water around them.

Catfish are named after the whiskers, called barbels, on their heads. These help the fish find food.

Sailfin catfish use their sucker mouths to pull algae from rocks and other surfaces.

Spines make the fins on their backs stand up. This makes the fish more difficult to swallow and puts off predators.

4 In another five days, they leave the burrow. They use their sucker mouths to grip surfaces, mostly resting during the day and looking for food at night.

3 In ten days, the eggs hatch into larvae. These tiny, see-through fish stay in the burrow, protected by their father and fed by yolk sacs attached to their bodies.

Sailfin catfish can live for 15 years if they reach adulthood. They have many predators, not all of them fish . . .

Piranha

When a school of red-bellied piranhas attacks, thousands of sharp teeth strip the flesh from the prey in seconds. These fish eat any meat and will sometimes attack young or injured birds.

1 The male piranha makes a bowl-shaped nest with its tail and swims in circles over it to attract a female. She lays about 5,000 eggs, he fertilizes them, and both fish guard them.

2 After a few days, the eggs hatch into tiny fish. They hide among the plants, feeding on the yolk sacs attached to their bodies.

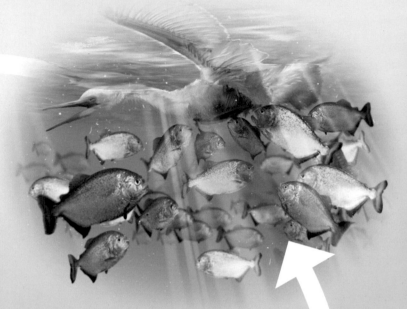

4 The toughest fish in the school lead an attack. Other piranhas sense the splashing, blood, and noise and join in, so large prey is eaten up quickly.

3 Young piranhas often take small bites out of the fins of other fish in the school for an easy little meal. This is called fin nipping.

Did you know?

Piranhas' teeth are razor-sharp to slice flesh off their prey. If one tooth breaks, a new one grows in its place.

The large, powerful tail pushes the fish's narrow, streamlined body quickly through the water.

Smell is more useful than sight for fish hunting in muddy waters. Piranhas also have sensors along their bodies to pick up the movement of prey.

Piranhas can live for five years, but they are not the only hunters in the water . . .

River dolphin

The river dolphin glides through the dark, muddy river water. It sends out clicking sound signals that hit prey, such as piranhas, and then bounce back. This tells the dolphin exactly where the prey is. Then it attacks.

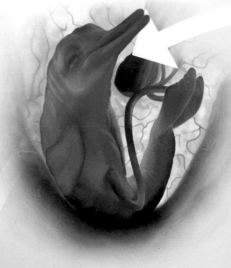

1 River dolphins mate every four to five years. A single baby, known as a calf, grows inside the female for 9–12 months.

2 The dolphin calf is born between May and July, when the river water is at its highest and there is a lot of food.

12

A river dolphin has 140 blunt teeth. The teeth at the front grab and crush prey, and the back teeth grind it up.

A river dolphin has a very flexible body and neck so it can twist easily between tree roots and search for food in hollow logs.

Dolphins breathe air through a blowhole on their head. The blowhole closes when the dolphin dives.

4 Adult dolphins may be white, pink, yellow, brown, gray, or black. They are always on the move, swimming up to 19 miles (30km) in a day.

3 The calf suckles milk from its mother for at least a year. After that, it eats solid food, such as fish and crabs. Parent and calf stay together for two and a half years.

River dolphins can live for 30 years. They have no predators, so they are at the top of many food chains.

Mayfly

Dark olive mayflies feed on algae in the streams and rivers of North America. They are sometimes called dayflies because they live as adults only for a few hours.

1 Females lay thousands of eggs on the surface of the water. The eggs quickly sink and settle on plants and rocks on the riverbed.

2 After a few days, each egg hatches into a nymph. It swims to find food and molts many times as it grows.

4 Adults fly up into the air in their thousands to find mates. They do not have real mouthparts, so they cannot eat. Once they have mated, they fall into the water and die.

3 After a few months, the nymph, now called a dun, rises to the water's surface. It has wings, but it cannot fly. It molts once more to get stronger adult wings for flying.

Did you know?

Mayfly nymphs grow gills, which they use to breathe under the water.

A male mayfly has large eyes shaped like turrets. They help it find a mate quickly.

Mayflies hold their wings upright, just like butterflies. The wings are see-through and very fragile.

The huge numbers of mayfly nymphs, duns, and adults make an easy meal for many other river creatures . . .

Brook trout

Brook trout live in cold streams and rivers and feast on mayflies. They are born in shallow streams, migrate to deeper waters, and then return as adults to breed.

1 In the fall, the female uses her tail to make a nest on the streambed. Then she lays up to 600 eggs and the male fertilizes them.

2 Within 100 days, the eggs hatch into tiny fish called alevin. They stay safe in the nest, feeding on the yolk sacs attached to their bodies.

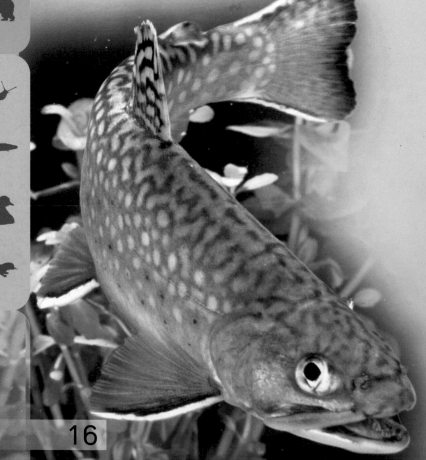

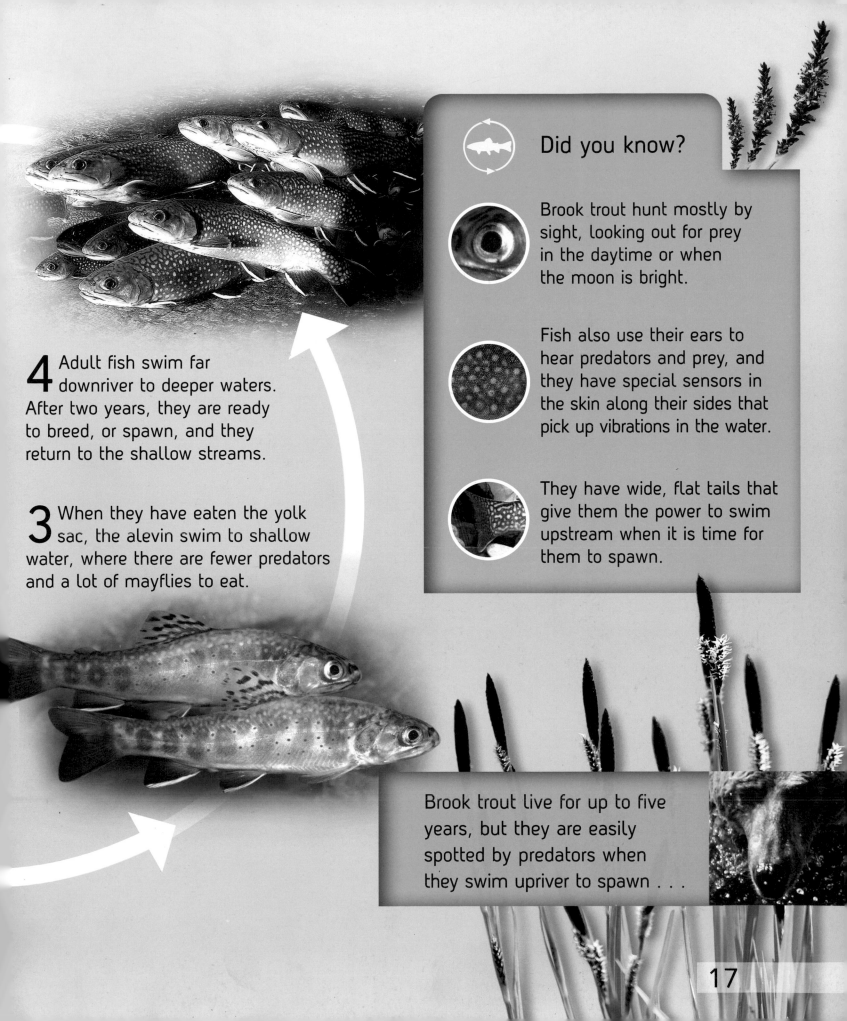

Did you know?

Brook trout hunt mostly by sight, looking out for prey in the daytime or when the moon is bright.

Fish also use their ears to hear predators and prey, and they have special sensors in the skin along their sides that pick up vibrations in the water.

They have wide, flat tails that give them the power to swim upstream when it is time for them to spawn.

4 Adult fish swim far downriver to deeper waters. After two years, they are ready to breed, or spawn, and they return to the shallow streams.

3 When they have eaten the yolk sac, the alevin swim to shallow water, where there are fewer predators and a lot of mayflies to eat.

Brook trout live for up to five years, but they are easily spotted by predators when they swim upriver to spawn . . .

Grizzly bear

Grizzly bears are furry giants that mostly eat plants. However, sharp claws and strong teeth allow them to feast on meat and fish when they can find it, including trout and salmon.

1 After mating, the female finds a den, where she hibernates for the winter. Here, she gives birth to two cubs. They are toothless and almost hairless.

2 The cubs' eyes open after six weeks. They feed on their mother's rich, fatty milk while she snoozes.

Did you know?

Long, curved front claws and strong legs are perfect tools for digging up plants and roots, as well as for grabbing fish.

A grizzly's large snout gives it a strong sense of smell that it uses to find food and to get to know its territory.

A grizzly's 42 teeth are not sharp, but they are perfect for chewing nuts, berries, and plants and gnawing meat.

4 Adult grizzlies mostly live alone, although they sometimes come together to catch fish migrating upstream. They can breed from the age of five.

3 In the spring, the cubs follow their mother away from the den. They will stay with her for about two years.

Grizzlies are most likely to die fighting one another. They are a top predator and can live for 30 years.

Great pond snail

Great pond snails live in ponds and slow-moving rivers across Europe. They stay near the water's surface, eating pond weed and scraping algae from rocks with their rough tongues.

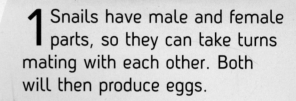

1 Snails have male and female parts, so they can take turns mating with each other. Both will then produce eggs.

2 They lay about 100 eggs on weeds and other plants. The eggs are held together in a special jelly, but many are still washed away or eaten by predators.

4 A pond snail has a lung for breathing air, but it can also breathe through its skin, so it can stay underwater for months.

3 Baby snails are born after about four weeks. Each baby eats the remains of its egg, which helps it grow a shell to protect its soft body.

Did you know?

As a snail grows, its shell gets lines on it. You can tell when a snail is old because it will have many lines on its shell.

The great pond snail eats grains of sand to help it break down tough plants that are difficult to digest.

Pond snails have tentacles with simple eyes at the ends that help them tell light from dark.

A pond snail can live for five years, but some animals love to eat its juicy body and even its crunchy shell . . .

Great crested newt

Newts look like lizards, but they are really more like frogs with tails. They are amphibians, able to live both on land and in water. Newts eat tadpoles and young frogs, snails, and insects.

1 Great crested newts mate in the spring. The female lays two to three eggs a day on underwater plants, up to a total of 250. She folds each one in a leaf to protect it.

2 It takes three weeks for a tadpole to form inside the egg. Then it hatches and feeds on algae and small animals, including other tadpoles.

4 Adult newts live on land but close to water, and they hibernate through the winter. They return to their birth pond to breed after three years.

3 The young newt has frilly gills so that it can breathe in the water. When it molts, the gills are replaced with lungs so it can live on land and breathe air.

Did you know?

Newts shed their skin all their lives. They sometimes eat the old skin when they have molted.

In the breeding season, males grow a tall, wavy crest along their spine and tail. This shows that they are ready to mate.

Newts use their tails as paddles to help them swim quickly through the water.

Newts can live for ten years or longer if they escape from the many dangers above and under the water . . .

Little grebe

The little grebe is happiest when it is in the water. This bird is clumsy on land but moves gracefully when it dives to catch prey such as newts and fish.

1 After mating, both parents build a floating nest, where the female lays up to five eggs. They hide the eggs under weeds if they have to leave the nest.

2 The chicks hatch, and the parents feed them tadpoles and small insects. Later, they take the chicks out onto the water, dropping prey for them to chase.

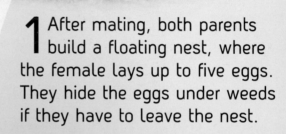

4 Adult grebes are excellent swimmers. They can stay under the water for almost a minute, traveling up to 100 feet (30m) as they search for food.

3 The chicks often ride on their parents' backs. Sometimes an adult even dives underwater with a chick still sitting there!

Did you know?

Little grebes have large feet with wide toes. They do not walk well on land because their legs are far back on their bodies and they find it difficult to balance.

A grebe can press its thick feathers close to its body or puff them up to change how high it floats in the water.

A long, pointed beak is perfect for snapping up and holding on to wiggling fish and newts.

Little grebes can live for more than six years, but fast-moving predators can catch and eat young ones . . .

Otter

Otters look cute, but they are deadly. Lightning-fast on land and in water, they chase down prey, such as fish and young or injured birds, and snap them up with their sharp teeth.

1 After mating, the female builds a shelter, called a holt, on the riverbank. It always has a tunnel underneath it so that she can slip straight into the water unseen.

2 About two months later, she produces a litter of up to four cubs. Blind at first, they open their eyes within a month and soon learn to swim.

Did you know?

An otter's webbed paws work like flippers to help it swim fast and turn quickly in the water.

An otter's body is covered with tough hairs coated in oil. Its skin never gets wet, however long it spends in the water.

Whiskers help otters feel vibrations. Even when the water is muddy, they can find prey without getting tangled up in weeds.

4 After a year, young otters leave their mother to find their own territory. They can breed when they are three years old.

3 Otter cubs suckle milk from their mother for four months. They learn to hunt by watching her and playing games with one another.

Otters live for only three or four years. They have no natural predators, but pollution in the water can kill them.

A European pond food web

This book follows two river food chains and one pond food chain. Most animals eat more than one food, however, so they are part of several food chains. There are many food chains in rivers and ponds, and they link like a map to make a food web.

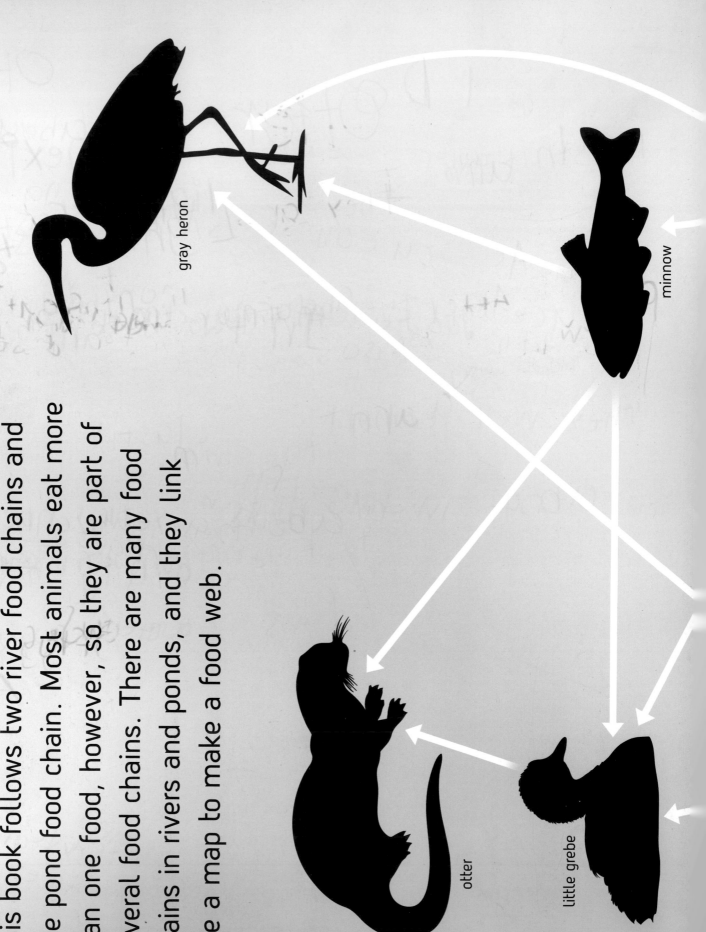

gray heron

minnow

otter

little grebe

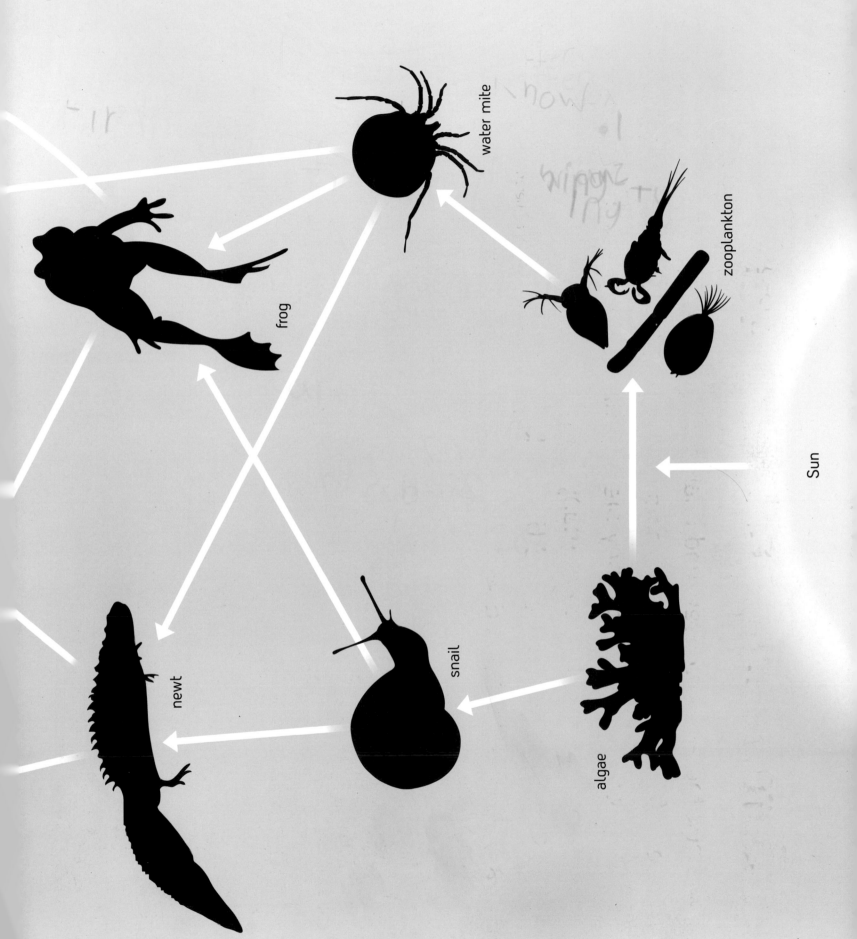

water mite

frog

zooplankton

Sun

newt

snail

algae

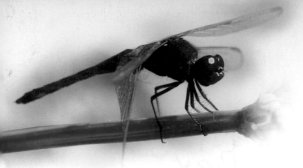

Glossary

ALGAE
Plantlike living things that make their food using the Sun's energy.

AMAZON RIVER BASIN
Part of South America where the Amazon and other rivers flow together.

BURROW
A hole or tunnel in the ground used as a shelter by an animal.

CONSUMER
A living thing that survives by eating other living things.

FERTILIZE
When sperm from a male animal joins with the egg of a female to make a new life.

FRAGILE
Something that is easy to break.

GILLS
What fish, newts, and mayfly nymphs use to breathe under the water.

HABITAT
The natural home of an animal.

HIBERNATE
To rest through the winter.

LARVA
A young insect that will change its body shape to become an adult. Groups are called larvae.

LITTER
A group of baby animals born to the same mother.

MATE
When a male and female animal reproduce. For some animals, this happens at a special time of year, called the mating season. Another word for mating is breeding.

MIGRATE
To go on a journey to a new habitat.

MOLT
When an animal gets rid of the outside of its body. This is also called shedding.

NYMPH
A young insect that is not yet fully grown and has no wings.

PREDATOR
An animal that kills and eats other animals.

PREY
An animal hunted by a predator.

PRODUCER
A living thing that makes its own food.

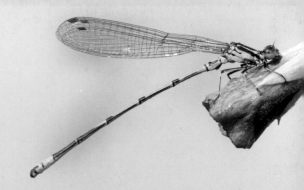

SCHOOL
A large group of fish.

SPAWN
When fish release their eggs to be fertilized.

SPINE
Part of an animal that sticks out from its body and is shaped like a needle.

STREAMLINED
When an animal is narrow and smooth to help it move easily through the water.

SUCKER MOUTH
Some fish have this type of mouth to help them suck algae from the surface of rocks.

SUCKLE
When a young animal drinks milk from its mother's body.

TADPOLE
The form of a frog before it is an adult.

TENTACLE
Part of a snail's body, used to feed and feel.

TERRITORY
The area where an animal hunts and keeps out rivals

WEBBED
When toes are connected together with thin skin.

YOLK SAC
A bag of food attached to a baby animal.

These websites have information about rivers and ponds or their animals—or both!

- ehow.co.uk/facts_5294605_common-newt-life-cycle.html
- kiddyhouse.com/Snails/snail.html#pondsnails
- kids.nationalgeographic.com/kids/animals/?source NavKidsAnimal
- nationalzoo.si.edu/audiences/kids
- thekidsgarden.co.uk/how-create-frog-friendly-pond.html
- video.nationalgeographic.com/video/player/kids/ animals-pets-kids/mammals-kids/pink-river-dolphin-kids.html
- zoobooks.com/virtualzoo .aspx?n=676484

Index

A
algae 4, 6,14, 20, 22, 29
Amazon River 6—13
America, North 14—19
amphibians 22

B
beaks 9, 25
bears, grizzly 18—19
beavers 4
birds 5, 8—9, 10, 24—25, 26, 28
blowholes 13
burrows 6, 7

C
calves 12, 13
catfish 6—7
chicks 8, 9, 24, 25
claws 18, 19
consumers 4, 5
cormorants 8—9
cubs 18, 19, 26, 27

D
dens 18, 19
dolphins, river 12—13

E
eggs 6, 8, 10, 14, 16, 20, 21, 22, 24
Europe 20—29
eyes 15, 18, 21, 26

F
feathers 8, 9, 25
feet 9, 25
fish 5, 6—7, 8, 10—11, 13, 16—17, 18, 19, 24, 26, 28

food chains 4, 5, 13, 28
food webs 28—29
frogs 22, 29

G
gills 15, 23
grebes, little 24—25, 28

H
herons 28
hibernating 18, 23
hunting 8, 9, 17, 27

I
insects 5, 14—15, 22, 29

K
kingfishers 5

L
larvae 7
lungs 21, 22

M
mating 8, 12, 15, 17, 18, 19, 20, 22, 23, 24, 26, 27
mayflies 14—15, 16, 17
meat 10, 18, 19
milk 13, 18, 27
minnows 28
molting (shedding) 14, 23

N
nests 6, 8, 10, 16, 24
newts, great crested 22—23, 24, 25, 29
nymphs 14, 15

O
otters 26—27, 28

P
pelicans 5
piranhas 10—11, 12
plants 4, 18, 19, 22
predators 5, 7, 11, 17, 19, 20, 25, 27
prey 8, 9, 10, 11, 12, 13, 17, 24, 26, 27
producers 4

S
sensors 11, 17
smell 11, 19
snails, great pond 20—21, 22, 29
Sun 4, 29
swimming 8, 13, 14, 17, 23, 25, 26

T
tadpoles 22
tails 10, 11, 16, 17, 23
teeth 10, 11, 13, 18, 19, 26
trout, brook 16—17, 18

W
water mites 29
wings 8, 9, 15

Y
yolk sacs 7, 10, 16, 17

Z
zooplankton 29